UnOrthoDox PaRaDoX

Poems, Prose
Or just my rambling thoughts…

By

Arrie Lane

Copyright 2025 by Arrie Lane.

All rights reserved. No part of this book may be used or reproduced, in any manner whatsoever, without written permission from the publisher.

ISBN: 979-8-218-76101-1

Dedication

To every being I have encountered;
Thank you for sharing space with me. To connection, even in differences. To you reading this right now. You are seen. You are Heard! You are Felt. You are Loved. You matter! Thank you for being you! May you find yourself amongst these pages.

Arrie

Foreword

I have started and stopped this book more times than I can count. Life, fear, perfectionism—one reason or another always stepped in. What you're holding is a culmination of past and present pieces of me: my work, my thoughts, my truths.

If you take anything from these pages, let it be this: you can start exactly where you are, with whatever you have, and trust the journey; It's yours. It doesn't have to be perfect—your art just needs to be shared. It's not meant to live only inside of you.

So, allow me to share a little of myself. Welcome to my beautifully chaotic brain. The structure is a bit like me—intentionally everywhere. One of the greatest things I've learned is that there are no absolutes, only variables and perspectives. The universe is balanced that way. God is balanced that way.

Fear tried to hold this book hostage. Courage refused to let it.
 I pray you receive these words well. I pray you find perspective somewhere in these pages.

I'm welcoming you in.

It's time to **enter the paradox**.

Come as you are.
Take what you need.

Thank you for your support.

— Arrie Lane

I told myself I would
write today…

Not sure about what, but I figure if I at least move my pen I'd begin to say something. If I write long enough something will come….

Or am I just writing my thoughts? And wasn't that the goal?

To write

Something…

PARADOX

paradox noun

par·a·dox | \ ˈper-ə-ˌdäks , ˈpa-rə-\

: a *tenet* contrary to received

opinion

: *a statement that is seemingly contradictory or opposed to common sense and yet is perhaps true*

```
"A world of black and white
        is merely…
          Grey."

      -Arrie Lane
```

"Paradoxically though it may seem, it is nonetheless true that life imitates art far more that art imitates life."

Oscar Wilde

The Paradox of You

Table Of Contents

Buried Haiku	12
Haunting Hydra	15
Strip For Me	21
Empty	24
You Are Not Alone	27
Silhouettes & Shadows	32
Beauty	38
A Strangers Closet	42
Human	43
Certainty's Promise	46
Moon Flower	48
Vacay For a Day	51
Tanka Break	57
All of You	58
Portals	61
Take Two	63
Wading	67
The Insomniac's Midnight Oil	71
Writing in My Phone Again…	73
Purple Heart	77
Love of Hate	85

Four	87
Love or Hate?	90
A Love Poem?	92
Cycles Break	95
ApParent Growth	101
Karmic Tides	105
The Shape of My Love	108
My City	111
Little Bakery	114
The Animals	117
The Shape Of Your Joy	120
Tanka Break	121
Time & I	122
Giver Of Life	124
More Than a Season	129
Earth Years	131
Pantoum	136
Letters to…	*139*

Buried Haiku

Found myself today.

I don't know when I lost you
Or where.
Searched through pages of my life for clues
Only to find bread crumbs leading to a version, a version of you.
I mean,
Me.
That I can barely recognize
Thought I could find your truth written on lines in books and lyrics that only seem to fit you when situations do.
Cinderella, elevate your feet, would you?
This slipper is conditional
Kind of like how I treat you.
Buried you under relationships
Left you on the back burner
called it growth,

But you're the pea, and the princess in me has been wrestling to find peace. What happens when we peel back the layers?

Hidden in plain sight,

I wouldn't recognize you if I saw you.
Feels like there's a stranger in my house;
It's haunting how hollow her hollers have become,
How her shadows look so ghostlike,
How her smile belongs to someone else these days.
Funny how reclaiming your peace can be such irony,
How fragments come together and the story plays out differently,
How self aware you have to be to find joy in free.

-*Turns out...*

I was never lost-

Just hiding.
Fear can be like that.
I stopped playing hide and seek with destiny
Told the monster this bed of lies I tell myself; I am all out of vacancies.
Told the reflection in the mirror she is worthy.
Found freedom in living
Learned to appreciate the beauty in the breadcrumbs, moments can be.
How to swing with the pendulum
Now I'm swinging into my blessings
of 20 plus more,
Unearthing the *buried haiku* of me.

Haunting Hydra

My body is a haunted thing that cannot tell the difference between its host and intruders.
Its protection is an overzealous cop,
Attacking first asking questions later
And me,
Well, I'm a dragon guarding the doors to this place.
I do not welcome many in for fear they will mistake my ghosts for me,
Label me a dead thing walking
Or call me my ghosts.
I prefer
They call me the Dragon that would not die.

Diagnosis-Hidradenitis.
I was 14 when my life changed,

When I learned the true meaning of
feeling like a stranger in my own skin.
Mine had betrayed me and I couldn't
fathom why.
An auto immune, auto inflammatory skin
condition with little research and very
few treatments.

I've seen more hospital beds and E.R's
than I care to count.
Tried every treatment you could think
of,
Been cut on more than I'd care to be.
Albeit necessary.
My body,
a mutilated sanctuary I struggled
praising in.
No cures in sight
only management.
So I managed
To love her in her brokenness

Searched her for wholeness
Convinced her of her worthiness;
To be loved
Even when I struggled loving her.

I learned to use joy as a weapon;
Smile the pain away.
Morphed my reality into a life worth living on days I felt like dying,
Turned tear storms into rainbows…
Rode them into pots of gold.
Called myself rich even when I felt depleted.

28
Pyoderma (PG)
14 must be a magical number.

I met my second dragon while still learning to tame or slay the first one.

I wrestled with faith because I could not wrestle with my body,
Could not hug her pain away.
Counted my days by counting my blessings because I needed something to hold on to.
Bandaged my wounds in hopefulness,
Wished upon ceiling stars
Lulled myself to sleep in opioid induced hopes of rest,
Propped myself up on walkers that felt like prison bars.
Told her
she was still worthy of all the love she gives.
Begged her
not to harden,
Prayed she would not quit.
Wiped her tears with it could be worse's
When I couldn't fathom what that looked like.

Called her a fighter even though she begged to retire,
Became a warrior in a war I never asked to go to battle in.
Now, Slaying two dragons.

The hydra Is a mythological creature.
It is said if you chop off one head
two more grow in its place.
I question if it was ever meant for me to slay these dragons.
Wonder
if they can ever be tamed.
I learned fire is its weakness.
How ironic
How the only way to tame these dragons is to become one unafraid to walk through flames.

So, I walk hoping to cauterize each head

Except my own …

It is said that Dragons represent
strength, power and good luck deemed
to the worthy.
If to whom much is given was a person,
It would be me in all my irony.
A walking oxymoron,
Both dragon and slayer.
A paradox,
All mythological and what not
But very real.

In this house we do not have to search
far for ghosts or dragons,
We simply wake up and attempt to slay
them again,

In hopes I do not slay myself in the process.

Strip for Me

The song goes…

**"Would you let me see beneath your beautiful,
Would you let me see beneath your perfect?
Take it off now! Take it off now!
I want to see inside.
Would you let me see beneath your perfect tonight?"**

The other day you got mad at me because you had dropped one of your hardest lines and my reply was, "Are you willing to strip for me?"
Now, I don't mean to offend but I've had my share of seemingly perfect 9-10's
But they were never willing to take it all off.

I need you bare.
Only there can our love truly blossom.
So, take off your mask of nonchalance.
Remove your armor and let me cradle your heart.
I need you to trust me with your pieces,
Not just a part but
ALL OF YOU!
So yes,
That means I want to love your darkness too!
You may not like it, but it gave me YOU.
Shaped you.
And for me to truly love you
I must appreciate everything that made you.

I long to meet the **Paradox of You**.
Like
Your strength,
From what weakness did it grow?

How does being vulnerable now make you impenetrable?
I asked you to strip for me because I want to see you naked.
However, these articles you remove cannot be held,
Only felt
By a soul as daring as you.
And Yes I'm scared too,
But if you strip for me
I will gladly strip for you.

So, may I have a peek?
Will you let me see beneath your "perfect"?
I long to see your purpose,
Your passions
Your fears
I want to see you in HD,
So, I'm going to ask you again,
Are you willing to strip for me?

Empty

Once jubilant
Filled with joy
Meets turbulence
Smiles no more.
Pockets too shallow
Somewhere, a wrong turn
Left heart hallowed
Fragile
Broken
Missing pieces
Nowhere to be found
Wounds left open
When?
Where?
How did it happen?
Answer,
Unknown.
This shell of a person
Only a house

No longer a home.

From weakness bore your strength. Through your darkness may you find your light. Purpose isn't about perfection, but rather it's about embracing what makes you different. Your uniqueness is in fact your purpose yearning to take flight.

So Fly.

You Are Not Alone

I didn't write this poem for you
I wrote it for the little child inside;
The one that is hurting,
The one you try to hide.
But not even the most beautiful smile
can disguise what lies behind the eyes.
That child is still searching for the
answer to one of the two questions that
really only matter:
Why?
Why me?
Why my life?
Why do I feel like a failure even though
I've tried?
Why don't I fit in?
Why does my success feel like a loss
When it's really a win?
And why do I still feel alone in a room of
my friends or next of kin?

Followed by,
Who am I?
Am I great?
Am I weak or am I strong?
Because I've been carrying this burden
of life too long.

I didn't write this poem for you
I wrote this for the person I don't know.
The one who lives in the shadows,
In your shadow.
But every time the light shines I get a
peek,
And contrary to popular belief it doesn't
make you a freak.
See, I see what lies beneath.
We all have shadows
The person we don't want the world to
know,
But no matter where we go

it follows.
So it would seem we can only escape
who we are in the dark
But that leaves us hollow.
I didn't write this poem for the you
I know.

I wrote it for the soul…
The one that has suffered many
heartaches and heartbreaks,
has been rejected and abused,
USED!
The soul that is confused,
The soul drowning in insecurity
Surrounded by obscurity,
The soul clinging to all the hurt and it
won't let go.
I didn't write this poem for the you I
know;

I wrote for every one of your flaws

And every one of your scars,
Because to me that's what makes you beautiful!

And to you I want to apologize
Because nobody sees beyond the eyes,
Or at least no one's tried.
I know I haven't tasted every tear that you've cried.
I know you're afraid to show the world who you are inside,
But I want you to remember
every ocean has a tide.
Remember that shadow looming behind
Cause God gave you a shadow to show you who you are and from where you came,
But as you look down at it let it remind you that you are still standing.

I didn't write this poem for you
I wrote it for the you I don't know.
The you that lives in the shadows,
In your shadow.
I wrote it for every tear and every fear,
For every triumph and defeat,
Both outward and internally.
I wrote it because
You remind me so much of me.
I wrote it for all of the unknown
To remind you that you are beautiful,
You are strong,
But most importantly,
To remind you that **you are NOT alone!**

Silhouettes & Shadows

In the dark we find our light.
Silhouettes and shadows
Silhouettes and shadows…

It's dark here
I keep bumping into shit.
Trapped in the mystery of darkness,
Running from pieces of myself
I'm not quite ready to deal with.
They say time heals all wounds,
But time ain't healed shit!
Just left me with a bunch of bumps and bruises
And a few open wounds.
It's funny, I've got a few locked rooms
I'm too afraid to visit.

I've been seeking out the light for a minute but,

I'm always bumping into all the wrong shit.
Showing all my weaknesses
all my imperfections,
Coming through my windows leaving these scary projections.
Maybe I'm crazy,
But right now,
Living in the dark seems to be my only protection.
Whoever thought I'd be afraid of my own reflection.

Reflecting on how I lost my direction,
Caressing my ego
Debating how much light I should let in today.
Am I ready to face my imperfections?
In this darkness I found a note left by the person before me,

It read,
"Stop hiding. Take a deeper look. I promise it's not as scary as it seems!"

I take a closer look around
saw some building blocks before me.
They all said different things
Like,
Love and loss,
Sickness, forgiveness, broken hearts,
Depression, trials, triumphs…
Lost friendships, lost cars, lost jobs, lost dreams…

I paused for a moment,
Then kept building
Strength, courage, wisdom, faith, stability…
Truth, freedom, dividends, success
Restoration completely!
Better health, better friends,

BETTER ME!

I took a step back once my building was complete,
And as the light crept in
I couldn't quite make the image out, but I saw beauty.
I looked a little closer
And to my surprise,
It was me!

I was no longer running from my shadows,
I had to learn to admire the silhouette that shaped me!

In the dark we find our LIGHT!

Silhouettes and Shadows!

She was. He was. They were….
A beautiful paradox. Both collected and in disarray. An open closed book. Logical, yet irrational. Tamed Chaos. Both Beauty and Beast. A lock searching for its key.

The key to life's mysteries…

Many of us are afraid to be our authentic true selves for fear of judgment, but what makes us different is also what makes us alike. Each snowflake has its own unique composition and yet they fit together like a perfect puzzle.

*We are alike because we are all different.
Uniquely you and yet still HUMAN!*

Still Beautiful. A sight to behold.

Beauty

Beauty.
I realize I don't fit your cookie cutter image,
And my waistline could account for all your measurements.
My hair- not straight enough.
Curls- not loose enough.
My morphing melanin confuses you.
I'm not your Covergirl
And it would seem all the Maybelline can't save what I was born with.
But despite your esthetics,
My smile is still beautiful, though it ain't perfect.
These curves are still a reminder to pay attention.
This 4C hair growing from my scalp doesn't need your extensions.

My beauty doesn't need to meet your requirements.

Your requirements have sent people like me into depression.
Caused more eating disorders than acceptance,
Caused less checkups and more surgeon visits.

I got so used to your rules
one day I looked in the mirror and could barely stomach my own image.

I wanted to be like you:
More make up
More cinchers
Straighter hair
Less obtuse,
More slender.
More…

Beautiful.
But it was never enough.

It never ends.
Smaller waist,
"Hmm, you need boob enhancements,"
Face done up,
"Now if we could just close that gap in."
You lied to me!
You told me this was beauty.
But every time I feel close,
You become distant.
You said this was beauty,
But all you meant was
Less me,
Less confident,
Less authenticity.

I should thank you though.
You taught me a valuable lesson.

You taught me no matter how you dress
up the outer appearance
It doesn't fix what's within it.
You must first accept yourself and all of
your blemishes.
The "Aha!" moment though,
Was when I realized I make you!
You don't make me.
Beauty.

A Strangers Closet (Dizain)

Clothes just don't fit me the way they used to;
My closet filled now with a stranger's clothes.
I'm due for a restock, dread the sort through.
I'm not who I was, came far I suppose,
Dysmorphia makes it hard to see growth.

I Appreciate the acknowledgement
But still struggle relishing in my wins.
Somedays my reflection still teases me.
I question if my reflection is fiction,
My eyes always lie, I'm trying to believe.

Human

They want you to apologize for being
human as if **feeling** is a burden.
Suck it up!
You're not tough enough!
They see your scars and condemn you
for not covering them up.

They want you to apologize for being
human,
As if **ONE** of the **FIVE** senses isn't
touch.
Forgetting the fact that when you **touch**
You **feel stuff...**
(Isn't that the point?)

They treat you like an alien because you
were brave enough to heal some stuff,
Look your **feelings** in the eyes and kill
some stuff.

Like bravery never grew out of fear,
They call you a coward, but it's their
cowering that got us here!

"How dare you be human?" they said.

How dare you **feel!**
How dare you admit that you still have
some wounds that haven't healed,
despite the bandages of denial!
How dare you!
Why are you crying?
Can't suck it up and ice your bruises?
Who told you to feel?

Didn't we tell you to place your emotions
in an icebox with a padlock?
Ship that shit off to a place you couldn't
find even if you wanted to,
And keep your return label so it can't be
returned to the sender!

Place a guard around your heart with some wires made of barb,
A few rabid dogs and a sign that reads,
"DO NOT ENTER."

They use Euphemisms to play down your truth, infusions and growing pains.

Pains growing and infusions truth,
Your "downplay" to euphemisms use.

THEY
Can't handle you **feeling** because they can't handle your healing,
Because then they would have to admit
That they **feel** too!
They'd have to admit that they're just like you;
Feeling shit,
Like humans do.

Certainty's Promise

At night
Tomorrow whispers sweet nothings of
todays in my ear
Lulls me to sleep
Welcome's me like Phoenix from Ash
each morning
There's something about time
How day morphs to night
Night into day
They say God is perfect that way
Seed
Flower
Caterpillar
Butterfly
Phoenix like
Metamorphosis
Proof change is inevitable
Proof Growth is always possible
Roses from concrete

Doesn't need explanation or reason
Just is

Moon Flower

Heard you ain't smiled in a while,
Heard it's been so long you barely
remember how.
Heard you thought yourself too tattered
to be beautiful.
That happiness was a gift that you
hadn't earned.
I heard darkness had become your new
home
With very little light to depend on.

Heard you cry more than you laugh
these days.
Heard it's been months since anyone
has seen your face.
Heard you've been searching for
Sunday's grace in a bottle,
Heard you found yourself at what feels
like rock bottom.

I always thought you a caterpillar though,
And see, I think you've mistaken your chrysalis for a prison, but I get it.
It's hard to see the light in the **dark**.

Hard to be growing into who you are while the world is passing you by.
Hard to feel stuck in a space and still feel alive.
I bet you thought you were living a lie.
Bet you thought your purpose had died,
Bet you thought yourself forever a caterpillar, never to be a butterfly.
See, you call it <u>buried</u>,
I call it planted.
You see <u>rain</u>-
Me, nourishment.
It hurts, I know
I get it.

Growing Pains

I heard you found yourself blossoming.
Then I wonder,
If flowers ever really know that they're blooming,
Or do they just find themselves surrounded by darkness,
And are they simply reaching for the light?

Vacay For a Day

There are all these expectations of me:
To be light bearer and way maker
A reincarnation and carbon copy
To be bold and docile-
And do it all with a smile,
But weights in water will surely drown you.
I have not perfected swimming against the current.
Somedays I am washed up on the shores of indecision
Hoping for resuscitation,
Others I am swallowed in the current.
Most days I am seen drifting,
Being carried
They do not check to see if I am breathing.
Or just there,
Me just being there be enough,

But somedays I too need a life raft.
Maybe today I needed light for me,
Perhaps I was trying to come back this time as my own savior.
I didn't want to be the bar today,
I just wanted to conquer the day.
I just wanted a hug,
Or to be asked what do you need, and somebody mean it.
I wanted to cry and not feel guilty for feeling,
But there is never enough time for me.
They say we all will sleep when we die, but I just keep coming back as somebody else's rest and refuge.

So today, I woke up late-
Ignored every phone call and it felt good.
I cried in the shower
I made my own waves

I was the current
I was reckless and careless
Brewed some tea
Rolled me one
Sat in my nothing
Floated away and did not care to anchor
I was kid free
For a moment, I wasn't mommy
or sister
cousin
aunty
friend;
I was not mentor or role model.
Did not have to be example
I poured Jack Daniel's
Drank it Neat.
I hugged myself
Saw the notifications and said f*** those emails.

Turned tunes on and the living room
was Madison Square Garden.
A one woman show,
Ending with a twerk session,
Blank trances into blissful nothingness
And I loved it.
Today I was selfish.
I opted out of counselor and consoled
self.
I was intentional about reserving today's
energy to just me-
It was nothing personal,
Just PERSONAL.
I gave myself permission to be
unapologetic for choosing me today.
Maybe I worked through some shit
Maybe I didn't,
Either way I'm cool with it.
Today I didn't care
About shit
On purpose.

For a moment
Damn it felt good.
Thought about tomorrow and decided it
will come with its own shit.
Rested in the present
There is peace here.
This f*** it energy seems necessary
I should visit more often.
I suppose, at least I'll always have
vacations.

*Some days I am not sure if I am the Beauty or the Beast.
Perhaps I'm both.
Maybe I'm just a beautiful beast or a beastly beauty.
Caught in the paradox of it all.
Maybe I'm just a matter of perspective.*

Tanka Break

Each dawn we rise up
Refreshed from yesterday's weight
We breathe in new air
It is fresh, ready, greets us
We walk till dusk and repeat

All of You

I love you as you are,
as you shed,
as you blossom,
grow,
as you become!
I love you shattered,
Mosaic pieced back together.
I love your colors.
Your pieces.
I love your cracks and jagged edges.
I just love how your story paints you a masterpiece.
I love you learning to Master your peace!
I love you WHOLLY!
I mean shot by life HOLELY because I realize it's those same shots that make me love you like you're HOLY…
Ascension,
sent here for me to love.
I love your light and dark,
I admire your shadows.

We all got demons; I love you back to
your angels.
I love you lost, then found, then lost
again.
I love you, hardened and cold.
I love you weak because it looks like
strength to me.
I love you limping, but still moving,
I love you stuck.
Yes, I love your beauty, but I also love
your beast.
You call it ugly; I call it misunderstood.
I love your flaws because they make
you unique.
I love you humpy dumpy
Phoenix from ashes
Renaissance
Building block.
I love you scarred,
Bandaged,
Healing.
I love you
even when you don't love me,

Because my love isn't contingent on
yours,
It simply is.
I love you endless
Infinite
Individually
And accordingly,
Like you're you
and I'm me
Only expecting you to be you.
It's easy to love your beautiful, but when
I say I love you,
Know that I love your ugly too.
Know that I don't only love a piece
I love all of you.

Portals

They say the eyes are windows to the soul,
That pupils be rabbit holes of emotion.
I have both found myself and lost myself in them.
Have seen more unsung songs
Untold stories in their stares,
They have served as gateways,
Windows into the Netherland
Landed me on mountain tops and shown me valleys.
It's funny how a gaze can be so,
penthouse view,
So, waves against sunset.
Some days that gaze be safe place.
Be clarity
Be peace
Be sanctuary
If your eyes could talk,

I mean create sound waves
They would wash up against the
shorelines of your mask of body
language.
They would carve away the truth in your
words.
Crazy how our eyes be both paint brush
and bare canvas.
How they be the beauty in the chaos,
Diamond in the rough
Encyclopedia of US,
And ain't that beautiful?
Ain't that connection?
Ain't that a sight for sore eyes?

Take Two

I'm listening to a dope 3 stacks (Andre 3000) track. New Blue Sun. It still feels like him to me. Still no deep thoughts.

My brother bursts out of the house. He didn't see me.
I say nothing.

Music is still playing. Upon his return he is startled. We laugh.

Is this still considered writing?

Speaking of Andre 3000

Thoughts as I listen. Yes, I wrote my thoughts.

1. Is it crazy to say I still hear Andre in the chords?
   Is this proof that some artists are felt?

   More than bars.
   More than just a voice box?

   When he titled the track, "I Swear I Really Wanted to Make a 'Rap' Album but This is Literally the Way the Wind Blew Me This Time,"
   This song felt like an earnest cry.

Like, "I hope you hear my heart.
I'm sorry. I choose me, but I love
you. I hope you understand."

Not gone, but rebirthed.
Why can I hear him like bars over
tracks when there are none?

Will revisit later…

Revisiting the past allows us to see our growth. I have learned to visit only when necessary. I do not stay long these days. It has far less to offer when I linger. That said, I have connected many dots through reflection. I have learned overstaying leaves more questions in a place that does not hold the answers. Only being present will. So, I walk and I write. I write and I walk. I circle back when I am called.

Rinse.
Repeat.

Wading

Some days my only peace is my poetry.
Others,
I can't find my poems,
Which means I can't find my peace.
These days I struggle to find the words
to articulate my feeling.
Don't know the proper metaphor for "I
am not okay."
Cannot find the right literary device to
drive myself home.
Home becomes a distant coastline,
My emotions a sea
Me,
Driftwood
Mind waves thrashing
Tossing me to and fro
And I am just trying to find
the calm.

But I am not Poseidon-
Somedays I do not feel Orisha,
Cannot summon my inner GOD.
The words don't form
I become a manic Stan storm,
***"Tea's gone cold, I'm wondering why
I got out of bed at all, morning rain
clouds up my window and…"***
I become aquatic,
Fish in the current.
Who knew cascading waterfalls would
save me
Carry me
Carve away pieces of me,
I'm just trying to find my peace…

Be still.

Mother Nature is teaching me how to
wade in the waters,
Reminds me I do not control the current-

That I cannot play GOD,
That GOD be living water.
There's no need to panic, I am not
drowning here.
Like waves,
This too shall pass...

So on the days I can't find my poetry
Or the words to articulate what I'm
feeling,

The right metaphor or Literary device
I open the flood gates.
Let heaven wash over me
I become one with the waters because
GOD be in the waters and I be of GOD.
An ecosystem is balanced
Equal part storm and Paradise.

Eventually...

Words will wash up against the
shorelines of pages again.
Lips will form waterfalls
Living words will cascade out
Both pouring and wading
Washing up against Life's shorelines.

I'm learning to find peace in this
process,

That some days will feel like storms, and
I will hope for words
Only to be met with eyes filled with
waters looking to return home again.

On these days
I figure I am just wading,
But still here.
And some days
That is peace enough.

The Insomniac's Midnight Oil
(Paradelle)

I burned the midnight oil
I burned the midnight oil
Wired, I did not lose form or blink once
Wired, I did not lose form or blink once
Midnight did not blink once
The wired form burned oil I did not lose

Procrastination has never been my kind of lesson
Procrastination has never been my kind of lesson
Only a fun not so distant friend
Only a fun not so distant friend
Procrastination has never been a distant friend,
Kind of my only not so fun lesson

Hate missing sleep, but love the product
Hate missing sleep, but love the product
I'm sure starting labor early is helpful
I'm sure starting labor early is helpful

I'm sure sleep is helpful but hate starting early
Love missing the product labor

My midnight labor is oil, the helpful form
Procrastination been my love/hate friend
I'm not early, but never missing a product
My fun lesson
Blink once, I'm sure I been wired
I did not sleep friend

Writing in My Phone Again…

So today I'm writing poetry about losing my poetry on my phones,
In my phone;
It's the irony for me.
It's giving insanity
And yet here I am proving some sort of point to myself.
But not really,
It's just I don't always have a pen and paper handy,
And rarely simultaneously.
Either I have the paper but no pen or the pen and no paper.
Honestly, I prefer the pen;
Anything can become a notepad.
Or I could just get this shit out as quickly as it comes.
Allow myself to become one with these words,

Stream of conscious this painting really quick
In its rawness.

Now I work hard to back my shit up.
My backups have backups and even then, I'm moving over to printing everything
Cause losing your art can feel like losing everything.
So, I etch every word into my memory,
But some days my memory gets shaky.
Got portion's missing
I won't lie,
Sometimes I like the challenge of performing new acrobatics,
linking thoughts with metaphors,
anchoring them in imaginary.

See how thoughts become poems
As quickly as they come?

So really, I'm just writing a reminder to myself.

Don't be careless with your words;
They be sacred
Make sure they live
You can't get them back
So, if they must be written,
Preserve them,
In more than just the mind.
The mind ages.
It may one day forget,
But on these pages
They live.
At least for now…

Written in my phone
Again.

There is no Hate if there is first no LOVE!
Only an emotion strong enough can cause such an opposing feeling.
So perhaps we do not hate at all.
Maybe we just love deeply...

Purple Heart

He loved her black and blue

Like fractured egos and broken bones

She knows it ain't right, but he told her he loves her

And she believed him

She's addicted to the way he showers her with love in public

See they've got the perfect image

He's the master magician and she's the lovely assistant

He taught her how to do magic tricks

Together they were master illusionists

He taught her how to paint on her smile

How to pull compacts out of hats like rabbit tricks

She learned how to walk a tightrope because of him

She knew if she failed, what the repercussions meant

She was his show girl

Go on give em a show girl

But now she's worn out

Spending her nights planning a way out

Can't tell you how many times she's packed her bags

Got the door cracked and heard

his voice in her ear and *stopped dead in her tracks*

Who gon love you like I love you

Who else gon want you

Leave me and swear to God I'll kill you

But his I love you's

sound like *a SLAP*

SMACK

a VERBAL ATTACK

Looks like dodging JABS

Sounds like, *"You're stupid!"*

Looks like, "You're dumb..."

Feels like a dead end job with limited benefits and no vacation

Looks like a bottle

Smells like a skunk

Looks like, "you're drunk!"

Acts like a b—h!

Looks like a
punk

PUNCH

BLACK OUT

                                      Feels like
                    a STRANGLE

           SUFFOCATION

                    she can't BREATHE

     like prison

                    she can't LEAVE

                        Looks *black and blue*

                        Feels like *it's bleeding*

                        Looks like *broken hearts*

                        Feels like *he needs me*

Looks like a nightmare

Feels like she's dreaming

It's isolating

Dominating

Tears have formed rivers attempting to cleanse wounds

Lately she's been self- medicating

Using elixirs and pills to numb the pain like it's lidocaine

She's lonely

And afraid

Scared

Dead If she leaves

Dead if she stays

I Pray to God she gets the courage to leave one day

I Pray to God she gets the courage to leave

Before it's too late...

(A world)

"Without contraries is no progression. Attraction and repulsion, reason and energy, love and hate, are necessary to human existence."

-William Blake
"The Marriage of Heaven And Hell"

"There is no difference between love and hate"

- Ichiro Suzuki

Love of Hate

Why do we treat love like it's unwelcome
less it proves itself worthy?
You say I'm too happy
I say
I made a choice,
Decided today was going to be a good
day.
Today I'll have something to be grateful
for.

I can see the preconceived notions
stitched into your skin.
I wonder if its thread is made of
judgment or conviction.
Funny, how we all wear our scars
differently.
Both self-inflicted
The irony
Audacious of me

Doesn't that make me a hypocrite?

But that is not the point of this poem
Or is it?

FOUR

Love time work
Stop
Work time love
Wait
Find lost self
Help
Give take
Even
With fear
step took
Make room gift
Made
Womb
Gave life
Both fast
Slow
When tear fell
Sink sunk
Swam

Drip ends with
Once upon time
Born Anew
Fall
Then rise
Eyes open
Won't quit

Fake seen with real lens
Rose tint gone
Don't fret
Press
Push
Till
Can't
Then rest
Rise
Push more
Walk
Into Open door
Free

From bags
That don't bear much seed
That grow
Just grow
Rain will come
Lift your head then,
Grow some more

Love or Hate?

Hate mirrors love,
Its opposition only validates its
existence.
The racist says he hates my pigment,
But bathes for hours in the sun hoping
for its richness.
They say my theory is flawed
That it has no premise,
But the acceptance of this truth is only
the beginning.
There is no up without down
No left without right
No day without night
No similarity without difference
Love then is only hates opposition.

When we look in the mirror
Reflected back is an image of our
likeness.

It looks back
Right's, now left's
The same but still
Different
Passion
Desire
Belief
Hope
Courage
Fear
Pain
Can you tell me the difference between
Love and Hate?
Because from where I stand its roots are
the same.

A Love Poem?

I don't usually write about love,
But I imagine it's finding $20 in the
pocket of some jeans you haven't worn
for years after you've emptied your bank
account paying bills.
Or maybe it's the rainbow after the rain.
Sometimes I think it's the questions we
can't quite find answers to.
A shifting variable.
I imagine love is every song we like, but
can't quite explain.
I imagine its rhythm cannot be counted
in 2&4 or 1&3.
It's more riddle than rhyme,
An inside joke,
Eye lashes that smile at you when
they're sleeping.
Strong like a typhoon but still calm like
an ocean

A wave washing against rocks.
I imagine all that
But I swear I don't write about love
But if I did,

I would write about you.
How you make me question everything I thought I knew about love,
How my dorky jokes found home in you
Cause I think I'm funny,
You think I'm funny.
I would write about your eyes and how I can see my forever's in them,
How your smile always feels like good morning
How your touch feels like safety
How your simple presence is intoxicating.

I promise I'm not a love poet
I usually don't write about love

But if I did I would write about us.
I would write about the day we met;
Our first date,
Our first kiss,
The first time I said I loved you,
The first time you said it back.
How we are a love poem;
A song,
Our very own love story.
How we are magic,
The answer to everyone's question.
How we are so,
Sunset over ocean,
How we are art;
Our own masterpiece.

Look,
I don't usually write about love
But I guess this poem is proof of another thing that love can do.

Cycles Break

I saw a child shatter once
Watched him break into pieces I wasn't
equipped to keep together
I was not super glue enough
Could not be answer to his questions
All broom and no bristle
And he a rug too full to be swept under
anyway
A collection of broken promises
And tears
And hopefulness
Clinging to every stolen moment
A pocket full of excuses
But a heart just as full of displaced love
and confusion
And anger
A storm I am never quite ready for
And I

can't anchor his expectations to reality
without damaging his spirit in the
process
He is always one Jenga brick away from
falling
I am always one stitch away from
broken safety net
And you...
You enjoy breaking things
Because you were broken once
Still a mound of unsolved daddy
mysteries
Another rug no one bothered to check
under
All shards
And blood
And stolen moments
And I
Am sorry Your son reminds you of all
the things you never had
But you would rather continue the cycle

I guess we only know how to break the things we were taught to
But what made you deem yourself a gardener?
Spreading seeds far and wide
Creating gardens, you never intended to tend to in the first place
He has your eyes
But his mother's heart
And I fear him becoming you everyday
But he becomes more like you and I everyday
But today,
He cried
And I let him
He spoke
I listened
We got a therapist
Because mommy ain't always mechanic
And that's okay
One day he will look at you

Features will mirror
But he will not see his reflection
Neither will you
Your heart will break
But he will end the cycle

So, my son is performing one of his latest hits and he comes to an end. The crowd of mommy goes wild! And that was all he needed to light up like Time Square. We embraced and my eyes began to water. I held him tight. I told him how proud I was. How amazing he was. And he smiled the biggest smile and said thank you mommy. How can a beautiful moment feel so heavy? As I tried to stay present, I watched him free, happy, smiling. I wondered to myself...

When is a black boy robbed of his smile?
When does it fade into reality?
When is his joy another fatality?

ApParent Growth

Children will grow you in ways you
never knew you needed.
They are the mirrors you can't avoid,
Reflecting both your beauty and your
beast.
They are patience,
Lots and lots of patience
Like,

If you were a stranger on the street you
wouldn't have the chance to test me, but
you're not, you're mine.
I realize you're still learning.

They are energy.
If you've ever been in a room with any
child, you know exactly what I mean.
They are felt.
Smiles that warm the iciest of hearts

Tears that pierce the hardest of souls
Joy that be infectious,
They are love.
Without rational reason
Because you are
Because you're growing
Because you need me
Because I just do.

They are compassion, empathy.
I love you's in spite of your flaws
because we are connected by a force
greater than just us.

And ain't it funny how we think we're
teaching them, but they're really
teaching us
On things we are sure we already get,
but have never been truly tested in.

That forgiveness is possible,

That we are all learning so perhaps we should be patient.
That we have all fallen so perhaps we should practice caring about each other's scars.
That we are all connected by something greater than just us,
That we should stop saying we are and practice stretching that muscle we call LOVE.
That we are capable of the purest form of love.
Our joy can feel rooms,
Our smiles can heal hearts,
That we can create bridges to the soul if only we believed it.
Children will grow you in ways you never knew you needed,

Ain't it funny how they teach us that we were never the teachers.

I remember, but I never told…

Karmic Tides

He said he just came to say sorry
Said he was searching for pieces of his manhood in her pain
Said he been reflecting on past transgressions
How he dropped bombs on her paradise after he pilfered all its precious resources never even thinking about its inhabitants.
Said he was selfish
Said she robbed him of all his diamonds
She-- not her.
He thought she was his new island,
Be he was hers.
Says he understands now
Says now he gets it,
Said he was hoping her tears tasted like candy,
But they only tasted salty, like regret.

Now his tears are someone's salty ocean
And he's just hoping for some forgiveness,
Not asking to stay on her land but to maybe plant a seed of healing for them both.
Said he never understood what it felt like to have sacred land torn up by a typhoon until his lands were destroyed.
Guess for him Karma wasn't a beautiful sunset on his soul's beaches.
Didn't taste like forgiveness
Didn't feel like freedom
Just like walking on shattered past-
Bleeding.
He said he just came to say sorry
For real this time,
but she don't believe him.

I once heard a poet say,
"There are no amber alerts
for the amber skinned girls."
That black girls go missing
without a whisper, and I
wonder if one day we will be
nothing more than mythical
creatures,
 nothing more than myths or
folklores used for
entertainment, but treated
like we never existed…

The Shape of My Love

They will tell you I am sweet & fiery,
That My love looks like I learned. Sweet
spirits are a fool's gold.
Society taught me that everyone wants
to be loved out loud, but quietly.
How kindness is cute, but love be
equally harsh, truth.
The medicine no one wants but
desperately needs
goes down harsh no matter how you
coat it with sugar.
Still necessary
Still anti-hero,
An act of rebellion and we all take a
stance depending on the day or journey.
Question its validity while seeking its
validation,
I am no stranger to its feeling.

I often go on love crusades,
A vigilante hoping to restore balance.
I was loved with correction,
Learned early on love don't always come in the forms we most need it.
It looks like showing up for yourself in rooms you hoped to see loved one seated in.
It's where I learned to be my own cheerleader,
And for my people I'm the whole damn cheer squad,
Yet I struggle being cheered for.

Imagine giving so much love but not being able to receive it-
Barricading yourself with it
To avoid its feeling.
A defense mechanism to ward off predators
I've been prey before,

All open and ripped apart;
I didn't like it,
So, I became a martyr.
Figured I'd die on this hill even if it be alone.
I'll be love even if love kills me.
Rebuild myself from its ashes
Build a wall
Perch love- rays atop,
Hope not to get hit in crossfire
Pray for peace
Prepare for battle,
Even if that battle is with myself.

My City

In my city
We don't say hello we say what up doe?!?
Moon walkin' to Michael cuz we keep finding the sunshine in our cloudy days.
We got helly GRIT
Hella faith
And I heard it through the grape vine that we be the auto pipeline.
So, it ain't a coincidence that we be the car & engine that keep the world running,
We be that joint that makes the thumb grip.
In my city
Ain't no north or south
Only east and west
And,

we know how to dress.
In my city
There's a difference between Vernor's and Ginger Ale
And yes, Vernor's is medicine.
In my city
We leave the country when we feel like it
In the same day.
In my city
Better made and Faygo is a culture
it ain't soda its pop!
In my city
And it's always acceptable to boss up and get this money while listening to Smokey.
In my city
You can travel the world a block away.
My city be the samples you find in hip hop
Be that reverb you hear echoed in rock.

In my city
Barry made a juice so sweet the whole world could taste it.
In my city we know that we're magic
Holy ground
Often imitated, but never duplicated,
From Belle Isle to Seven Mile and abound,
Ain't nothing like the D, like Motown.
We know it
And we're proud!

Little Bakery- Sestina

Who knew little hands could make you so joyous
That you would create order amidst the chaos
Tears are somehow swept away like crumbs
Suddenly strutting with a new bounce
Filled with such life
The world welcomes you like sunrise

When young children wake bright eyed at sunrise
They are hungry enough to eat, but always leave behind crumbs
They grow older and no longer find waking with the sun joyous
The process of growing up feels more like chaos
Gnarled fingers holding on for dear life

They search for new reasons to bounce

Discovering yourself starts as chaos
You learn to follow breadcrumbs
Action based, springing into to action...
bounce
At some point you learn to again
befriend sunrise
Catching Sun for fun becomes joyous
Life,

Smiles are found in life's crumbs
You, now a calm in the chaos
Walking with a new bounce
You become a reason to be joyous
Sow seeds of life
A sunrise

Your own bounce
Above the chaos
Less angry, more joyous

A beachfront view of sunrise
Bearer of light and life
You now understand how to make a
bakery of life's crumbs

A Poets Second Attempt at a Sestina

The Animals

Rooms love a good elephant
Enjoy them sneaking in like cats
Everyone howling like hit dogs
Prefer they actually just blend in, be chameleon
But their tongues lie like snakes
They be lion.

No longer running from the lion
We learn to walk with elephants
The truth hiding in corners, tongue held by cats
Match energy like chameleon
When truth is shut up in the esophagus, we do not use snakes.
No one acknowledge sleeping dogs.

We let them lie dog
We paralyze our victims, snakes
Trample spirits we become elephants.

We do not forget how they crept in like cats
They pretend to be wall flowers, chameleons
Making prey of ourselves they pounce on opportunities like lions.

We lack the full scope, we are not chameleons.
They pray we forget but we are elephants.
We keep the memories, digesting our traumas like snakes.
Holding on to the bones we pick as dogs.
Crafty cats,
We roar like lions.

Domesticated cats
We do not shape shift we just fit our environments like chameleons.
Have you heard the tale of the lion?
Bit by the snake,
Proof small things can be elephants

And we don't lay with dogs,

We train them to be chameleons
Bark them into a stampede of elephants
Gnaw them down to the bone like dogs.
Once ferocious lions,
Now frail cats.
We become slicker than the snakes.

The Shape of Your Joy- Decima

Your presence lights up every room
Embraces with arms wrapped tightly
Lips ajar, teeth shining brightly
Surely, darkness has met its doom

You pass smiles around like heirlooms
Like you've discovered the secret
This energy, never leave it
Made of rainbows rain left behind
You are the pot of gold, the kind
We join in with, without regrets

Tanka Break

I have met love once
I've made a home in its fields
Rested in its scent
It smelled of sweet lavender
Felt like a needed exhale

Time & I

I am a lot of things to a lot of people
I sometimes forget to leave room for
myself.
There's never enough time to make time
even if time be an illusion.
Each room, crack and crevice is filled
with something or someone or
something for someone.
I can't even squeeze in the seconds
before hands outstretched for
moments,
Tap on curved shoulder
and I will answer.
Maybe it's a trauma response.
Perhaps I know too well the feeling of
being left behind, wasted 1, 2 many
times
by 3,4,5

just as sure as time is a nonrenewable resource...
So am I.

Giver of Life

If the world ever deemed herself
godless
I'd believe her.
I'd wade in her waters
eat of her land
Trust her sun to light my path
And her stars to be Navigation system.
I'd recognize she never needed a deity.
That she lives
Breathes--
Only life comes from her so How could I
question her decision?
If this earth ever deemed herself
Godless
I'd believe her.
The first time
I'd act like
I've seen her wrath in her children:
Zeta, Florence, Harvey, Katrina.

How she wept floods over Dubai.
I've witnessed her fits and convulsions,
I know she will shake shit up if she must.
But I've also seen her beauty-
Tasted her fruit,
Danced in her fields,
Her mountains etched to pure perfection.
I have cried in her presence-
I'd probably call her Yah.
All praise be to the wind that whispers and howls.
I'd worship her waters
Dance in her streams
Baptize myself in her rivers.
I know a life giver when I see one.
I'd call her, this place be heaven, hell and the in-between.
Tell me,

Have you ever smelled her lavenders and lilacs?
Taken her medicine,
        Elderberries and ginger?
Ever seen her spring into action?
Summersault into fall?
Wintergreen and cold shoulder when she's resting
But she never leaves,
She simply cascades from trees.

I've met her creatures
Heard their songs
Hell, I've even hummed along.
Had revival sessions grounding in her grass
Found myself time again in her atmosphere,
And if I must fear the unfathomable,
She'd be suspended in a universe
Rotating on an axis

Connected to only energy,
Held by absolutely nothing
Yet somehow feeding us all.
She'd be my Alpha and Omega,
I'd study her tides like scripture
Like my life was in her hands
Like tomorrows aren't promised but
todays are!
If I woke tomorrow and there was no
God
I'm certain I'd praise the earth.
The most tangible proof of the intangible
I know.
We enter her presence
Walk with her daily
And when we leave,
We return to her.
There's something sacred about that,
How she be holy while holding me
Hopefully, she is pleased.
And since she came before me

And will likely be here when I leave,
I'd praise Mother Earth
The beginning and end,
The Genesis and Revelation.
A constant
Head bowed-
My two hands coming together.
Thank you
And Amen.

More Than a Season

Orange is beautiful against earth tones.
Some days I wonder if trees be kin
Of my mother.
Watch her morph like melanin
Watch her shed lining
Like she understands the point of this
period.
Like she knows when to bear fruit
Her apple bottoms fit hands,
Fills cup,
We sip and gallivant in her fields.
We find feasts;
She smells like cinnamon and nutmeg
Fresh out the oven.
She is a gentle reminder that
hibernation is not death,
That we all have a cycle,
That an object at rest may be an act of
self-care,

But she is never dormant.
Reminder to prepare for Wool coverings to morph into insulation.
That precipitation will soon turn crystal like, so boots become more than garnish.
Note to self a withering thing eventually Leaves,
But she'll be back again.
Each time I'm thankful.
Next time I may dress up,
This time I brought her an amber pie and greenery
Just to remind her of her beauty and necessity.
She thanked me for honoring her presence
I thanked her for her frequencies.

Earth Years

January.
In the beginning
There was only darkness and energy.
Space,
Cold and empty
But presence was with me,
And in February
Came seed.
But it's still dark.
In the distance I can hear a heart
beating like
reminder of whips lashing across backs.
As a matter of fact
I imagine energy created its first star in
March.
They say a star is just collapsed energy
So when my ancestors leave
And I look to the sky

it's no wonder those stars look kin to me
Like friend to me.

Felt gravity's pull in April,
As if time & space collided with fate--
and collapsed
creating a new place.

This place came out of darkness--
was warm;
I'm sure this was SUN.

They say everything happened at once,
but I think the stages of life need the
right space to form.
Like earth was a seed of the universe
first and then was watered, and she was
born.

So, when it rained,

it rained for days
And in May…
Was flower
Was life
Was me.
In June
They saw its beauty
Decided something so beautiful should be put on display,
Decided the only way to pimp it was to cut it away.
They had questions,
I had answers only my construct could say.

July,
I found myself in a lab
On life support,
Alive but barely breathing.
I look around I see my siblings,
In August they collapsed

Made mother so mad
she shook the ground
As if to say, "leave my children alone
now!"
In September,
she cried so much she sent floods.
Her wails howled in strong winds,

"Y'all ain't listening, so I hope you hear
this! Y'all are making me sick!"

October,
they told her
They get it, said they would only take
what they needed,
But they didn't they injected her with
toxic garbage,
Manipulated her seeds.

In November she got so sick,
Said she couldn't take it.

December,
She was shivering
Cold
But hopeful it would protect her
creations,

Because in the beginning,
There was only darkness and energy-
Space,
Cold & empty.
It is sad the world is just collapsed
energy,
But what happens when the source runs
dry?
When mother earth ceases to birth life?
When she ceases to cry,
Will we then apologize
or will we just ask why?

Pantoum

The same fire that warms you will burn you
Play where it's safe
No one is safe here, not even me
I dread every second we both become casualties

Play where it's safe
There is no room for error here
I dread every second we both become casualties
Victims of raging tongues

There is no room for error here
But we are both marked and marred
Victims of raging tongues
Ego splattered everywhere

But we are both marked and marred

A steel caged match there is no way out
of
Ego splattered everywhere
Me a blaze; both box and match

A steel caged match there is no way out
of
Play where it's safe
Me a blaze; both box and match
No one is safe here, not even me

Everybody's talking a
language few understand
Miscommunication paints
victims and villains
Or victim into villain

Letters To...

To the doctors who denied me pain meds,
Saying my blood was too green.
Ask me to put down the weed, but I only picked it up because my chronic pain took a back seat since drug dealers and shitty doctors didn't mind creating addicts with pill habits and somehow that fell back on me.

The first time I found myself feeling like I was begging y'all to help me. Proving my case like, "check my file, look at my history. I keep pills longer than need be," And they said to me, "Well how much do you need? *The fuck type of question is that?* And I say, "I don't know, but I'm really not interested in coming to the emergency If I can ride this out."

At this point I'm exhausted. I just say fuck it, I'll suffer through it.

Dear Doctors,
That toke don't always erase the pain, but it does allow me to escape it sometimes.
That may sound real vice-ish.
I'm woman enough to admit, it is.
But I got every right on days where the fight gets rough to light the fuck up.
Plus, I heard the side effects are less anyway.

And you may judge me-
That's cool.
Sometimes this J be the thing keeping me grounded,
That edible or oil be the only thing that cradles me to sleep.
Chronic pain is every day

And granted, some better than others,
But you haven't seen my sleepless nights,
Fought yourself to get out of bed
Painted on a smile for the world while holding back winces;
To long for a new normal.
But search for beauty in what seems to be ruin,
Guilting yourself for being selfish because there's somebody who has it worse.
At least you're here, be thankful.
Battling with allowing yourself to be human and say, "Damn, this sucks!"
Fucking right Imma blaze up.
And you know what, don't like it?
I don't give a fuck.

To the People Who Told Me Life ain't Sunshine, Bubbles & Daisy's....

My happiness is…
An armor and a weapon.
Maybe hallelujah in the midst of a storm.
To David, to let a Goliath triumph over me,
Don't you know a war cry when you hear one?
It is not an attack,
Comes in peace, but knows how to swing.
Doesn't owe you explanation,
My joy shouldn't make you so uncomfortable.
You should work on that.
It's a choice I choose every day.
I figured since I can't stop the rain, I may as well dance in it.

So, I be drenched, muddy as fuck but
still frolicking.
My happiness knows joy cometh in the
morning
So, it preserves.
Chooses to remember to count my
blessings, Like my family,
my friends, my life,
my limbs,
they all work,
and I might not have everything,
but I have what I need.
It's my son's hugs, just because.
How do you be free and sweet,
reminder of happy.
It's my people winning because I love to
see it.
When they win, I win.
So, my happiness is an applause for
them too.

It's gardening for the first time with my mom.
This beautiful work
When our thumbs weren't quite green,
we embarked on this beautifully bumpy journey.
Made a garden of our exhales
Rested in the peace of the process-
The harvest was worth the work.

Here, worries become Compost to the kind of fruit that doesn't need your validation as the proof of the shit it grew through.
What I'm saying is I don't owe you the compost of its composition.
Today it just fucking is,
And isn't that enough?

But you would rather me a bloody mess
than a bandaged wound; And I can't
fathom why.

It's conquering myself daily.
Isn't easy
Ain't for the weak
Is a full-time job
Doesn't owe its story
Or my traumas,

But you would rather me a bloodied
mess than a bandaged wound.

And I can't fathom why you're so mad,
my happiness has more commas than
periods. It's because it keeps me finding
shit to add to my gratitude list.
My joy is a run-on sentence, the song
that never fucking ends.
Because today, I woke up still breathing.

I had enough fight to get up and keep living.
Went to sleep a test,
Woke up testimony.
My happiness is that testimony.

Did you know that some days I don't feel "happy"?
Those days my happiness is that too,
It's the growth and comfort I find in being uncomfortable.
The beauty in the rain that I CHOOSE to see rainbow.

I know I don't wear my journey like you,
But just because I'm smiling doesn't mean I'm not fighting too.
I'm incomplete,
Always work in progress
but content with finding joy in this journey.

So, I guess this poem is called:
My happiness is...

All the things that make me
Me!

So yes, I am sunshine and bubbles.
Sunflowers
And daisies
Damnit! I'm a fucking daisy!
Blooming through concrete
And I like it.
And do you know what that makes me?
Fucking Happy!

Toxic people,

I am restricting your access.
I'm moving and you can't have my new address.

You're always popping up unannounced and breaking things,
Last time I let you in, you left my home a mess.
It took me months to bounce back.
Last time you couldn't come past my doorstep, so you stood on my porch making so much noise everyone came out to see,
Said you meant no harm-
Blamed my boundaries on me.
Said you were sorry, that it wouldn't happen again, then proceeded to burst out my windows leaving me to pick up the pieces
to clean up this mess you left, alone.

I am moving away.
My mind, body & spirit make my house,
But my PEACE makes it home.
And home should be a safe place,

Sacred haven
But no,
In you come, make a ruckus
            Clanging pots and pans,
Singing off key.

Understand, this wasn't easy for me.
I was just helping you clean up the mess
somebody left in your home last week.
But you can't follow me,
See they say burglars rarely are
strangers on the street,
That we are usually robbed by people
we know.
That we all got a Judas lying in our mist
who just wants to be attached gift to
your light, to what you can give, but
don't care about preserving it.

This isn't Kansas. Anymore.
Heard we all have a wicked witch

Heard the yellow brick road never got
Dorothy home,
Heard we all got Imposters like The
Wizard of Oz-
Heard her home was her mind.
I heard my home was my mind,
Is my peace.
That it's invaluable,
Priceless,
Should be protected.

And y'all, Dorothy gets back home...

A Letter to You and Your Boxes

Caution,
I'm a dreamer and I'm claustrophobic,
So boxing me in is hopeless.
How do you limit the limitless?
My presence is infinite:
Is light
Is gifted
Is luminous,
So if you can't handle this shine get some shades.
Want to box me in and use me for your benefits-
And I ain't interested.

An Open Letter...

Today when you wake up and start your day don't forget your empathy.
Leave the high horse at home you don't need it.
Remember your confidence, but don't forget your greatness is apparent, it needs no explanation.
Don't take things so personal.
Remember,
Guarded can look a lot like arrogance.
Don't forget we are all fighting our own battles.
Remember that often our battles miscommunicate our intentions, blur our vision, break our spirits.
Don't forget your transgressions,
Remember, they are your connection
Remember your imperfections

Don't forget we all got shoes no one else can fit.
Remember we all have a story
Most rarely get told.
Most of us feel misunderstood
Our truths rewritten,
So before you judge,
Remember you've paid mortgages on your own.

Glass houses put those stones down,
But don't forget understanding does not mean you have to agree. You're entitled to your opinion and so are they. Your up can be their down. Your dots can form a triangle and theirs a square.
Remember we all see through our own perceptions,
Don't dish more than you can take.
Remember you've been down your own rabbit holes.

Don't forget,
Your growth is not just in that you made it, but that you get it.
Remember most of us wear masks.
Don't forget you're still wearing one-
How dare you point out someone else's.
Remember vulnerability is scary so listen without judgement, we all need an ear.
Don't forget love is a life raft, mouth to mouth,
It disarms weapons of mass destruction.
Remember you are someone's light.
Be an example,
Most importantly remember you've met grace and seen mercy.
When you leave home today, please remember
Your empathy.

Be patient with the world,

They don't want you to pity or feel sorry
for them, they want you to understand.
Remember you too are imperfect
You too are human,
Just like them.
You're Still learning,
Still growing.
Remember you don't have all the
answers, It's okay.
Don't forget you can't save everyone, it's
not your job,
All you can do is offer your light.
Remember to grab a few logs on your
way out the door, somebody's fire is
dying, and they could use it.
Set healthy boundaries, know your
limits.
Be caring, but don't let others abuse it,
and when you come home and you
undress remember to take off other
people's burdens as well,

Don't take problems to bed.
Take some time
Clear your head
Unpack your own baggage
Write it all down.

Get out.
Give yourself permission to be flawed,
To be human.
Cry if you need to,
Allow yourself to have a moment
And when you finally close your eyes,
Remember, you are resting your head
on Mercy's pillow and bundling up in
graces comforter.
They get it, they understand,
And tomorrow when you rise again and
start a new day,
Please,
Don't forget your empathy.

I have not forgotten the ones
who counted me out. Clearly,
They miscounted…

To the Reader,

I hope today you smile so hard your cheeks hurt. May you feel an immeasurable amount of Love and Peace.
Regardless of who you are, what you've done…Where you're headed will be a collection of your experiences. Good and bad. Light and dark, The pendulum swings both ways. Love yourself through the storm. Your rainbow is coming. The Paradox says…It has to! If no one has told you lately, I love you and your presence on this earth is needed, valued & necessary! Your smile makes someone's day. Your existence on this earth is not by chance! You matter! You belong! You are LOVED!

Love isn't a band aid.
It's the stitch
holding us all together…

To Poetry…

Gramma's Gift

I fell in love with you
One afternoon in grandmother's living room,
But I didn't know it.
I was still learning to love myself...
Or maybe I was learning to love myself.
Didn't matter, it was like the 1st day of school and Gramma figured I could use a new friend,
So she introduced us.
I don't know if she planned for us to get this close,
But somehow, somewhere between becoming my enemy and my bestie,
I found more pieces of me in you than I ever expected to.
It's like you knew me before I even knew you existed.
Made my grandmother a historian and a prophet.
Poured architecture from her lips.

Creator of foundation when she brought us together,
She never worried about the bricks.
I guess she always knew they'd come.
Guess she trusted us to do the work
even if we parted ways.
Guess she trusted we'd always find our way back.
That her faith be breadcrumbs enough,
She always said, "Train up a child!"
Funny how my grandmother was a
Proverb wrapped up in a Psalms.
I think our meeting was prophesy.
Like, Grandma was just being obedient,
Like I was a part of her assignment.
Our connection be proof that even a mustard seed,
be seed enough
If planted
In faith
on fertile ground.
I guess grandma made me a revelation.

Gave me you as proof that gifts don't
always come in boxes with fancy bows
or wrapping paper.
Some days they look like sitting at
Grandma's feet, listening and learning.
Lord knows, some days we drove each
other crazy and we didn't always agree.
But somehow,
she knew you'd be a safe place.
Knew you'd help me find my way when
the path got hard to see.
My Grandmother was the bridge that
brought us together

Made me a Dorothy.
Called you The Wiz.
So, I guess I'll call her my yellow bricks-
Illuminating our connection.
When she left,
She became our personal constellation.
Pointed me to you,
Called you my North star.
It reminds me to thank her for
introducing us.

Reminds me,
We share her with the world whenever
we link up.
Reminds me,
We speak her sacred language.
That she was here, is here!
My Grandmother was a proverb,
wrapped in Psalms.
She spoke in stanzas
And she was all prose.
I was gifted her first name for my
middle,
Christine.
There she goes,
Bridging gaps again.
Being connection
like…
Like Poetry.
I think she was poetry.
I KNOW she was poetry.

In loving memory of my Grandmother
Christine Lane,
Thank you for giving me Poetry.

```
Let your Joy be an act of
  Rebellion and Alignment.
```

Unorthodox Paradox

Arrie Lane

Email
ArriesLane@gmail.com

📱 Instagram
@ArrieLane
@Detroit_Verses

🌐 Website
www.ArrisLane.com

🎥 YouTube
ArrieLane

Youth Services — NextVerse Detroit
NextVerseDetroit@gmail.com

www.ingramcontent.com/pod-product-compliance
Lightning Source LLC
Chambersburg PA
CBHW051129160426
43195CB00014B/2396